Improve your Spelling

Victoria Parker

Designed by Diane Thistlethwaite
Illustrated by Kevin Faerber

Educational consultants:
George Phillipson and Jane Davage

CONTENTS

Niether or *neither*? *Pursue* or *persue*? After using this book you will have no doubt which are the correct spellings. Don't despair if you think you are a bad speller. Although some find it easier than others, spelling is a skill that can be learned. The fun tests in this book will give you lots of spelling practice. There are also guidelines to help you avoid making mistakes.

User's guide

Each double page in this book focuses on particular spelling problems. Read through the summary of guidelines at the top of each left-hand page, then test your spelling by trying the puzzles which follow. The book has not been designed for writing in, so you will need some paper and a pencil or pen for jotting down your answers. You can check them on pages 28-32. Don't worry if you make mistakes. Just work through the book, then go back to the beginning and try again. You will definitely improve next time.

Watch out for boxes like this. These contain words for you to learn and test yourself on. Some will be new to you, so have a dictionary handy to check up on what they mean and how to use them.

Why is good spelling necessary?

Spelling is an important skill for many reasons. Above all, it is vital to be able to spell correctly so that you do not confuse your reader. For instance, there are certain words (called homophones) which sound the same, but which have different spellings and meanings.

The cereal was advertised on television.

The serial was advertised on television.

Other spellings are so similar that even a small mistake may make it difficult for your reader to understand you.

The desert was a generous helping of lemon meringue pie.

The dessert was a generous helping of lemon meringue pie.

As your spelling gets better, your writing style will also improve, because you will be able to write with confidence, using a wide range of words to express yourself.

Where does English spelling come from?

Modern English is a mixture of languages. Long ago, the Ancient Britons spoke Celtic, but over the centuries each of the peoples that invaded Britain contributed words from their own languages. For example, *skirt* comes from Old Norse, *index* from Latin, and *garage* from French. More recently, English has been affected by influences such as the growth of travel and trade, the World Wars and the rise of broadcasting. For instance, did you know that the word *shampoo* comes from India, *studio* from Italy, and *parade* from Spain? English is still changing today, in order to express new ideas and experiences.

q r s t u v w x y z a b c d e f g h i j k l m n o

USEFUL TERMS
What are vowels?

The five letters *a*, *e*, *i*, *o* and *u* are known as vowels. When *y* sounds like "i" (as in *sky*) or "e" (as in *jolly*), it is also considered to be a vowel. The other letters of the alphabet, including *y* as it sounds in *yes*, are called consonants. Each vowel has two sounds: short and long. Say the words below. The blue words have short vowel sounds. The red words have long vowel sounds.

hat   fence   stick   dog   mud

gate   tree   kite   bone   blue

What are syllables?

Many words have more than one vowel sound. Each part of a word which has a separate vowel sound is called a syllable. For example, *dig* has one syllable, *mar/ket* has two syllables, *ex/pen/sive* has three and *in/vis/i/ble* has four. Breaking a word down into syllables often makes spelling easier.

Try counting the syllables in the words on this shopping list, then check your answers with the ones on page 28. Don't look at the number of vowels in each word, as this can be misleading. Just say each word aloud, and count the vowel sounds you hear.

soap
toothpaste
detergent
bread
peanuts
macaroni
coffee
milk
eggs

honey
lemonade
cheese
tomatoes
cauliflower
onions
bananas
oranges

What is stress?

When you say words of more than one syllable, you usually put more emphasis on one syllable than the others. For example, <u>mar</u>ket, in<u>vis</u>ible, ex<u>pen</u>sive. This emphasis is called stress, or accent.

Read out the words on the shopping list again. Can you hear where the stress lies in each one? Check your answers on page 28.

What makes a spelling correct?

The idea of "correct" spelling is not very old. Until the 18th century, people spelled words however they liked. They even thought nothing of spelling a word in several different ways in the same piece of writing. When the invention of the printing press made written material available to large numbers of people, it became clear that spelling needed to be standardized, so everyone knew exactly what a writer meant. The first English dictionary was written by Samuel Johnson and published in 1755. But the patterns he defined were not always consistent or logical. So today, some words are more difficult to spell than others.

English has continued to change since then, as new words have entered the language and others have dropped out of use. Also, the spelling, pronunciation and meaning of some words have gradually altered. This is why there are differences between British, American and Australian English. You will find that a few words can still be spelled in more than one way (such as gipsy/gypsy). In these cases, use the spelling you find easiest to remember. But if you are surprised by a spelling, always check it. It may be misspelled, or even be a different word. For example, passed and past do not mean the same thing.

Vowel sounds are often spelled in unexpected ways. For example, a long "e" is spelled by *i* in *marine*, but by *y* in *tiny*. Also, many vowel sounds are spelled by two vowels together. For example, *tread* (short "e" spelled *ea*) or *float* (long "o" spelled *oa*). The most common ways of spelling vowel sounds are set out for you here. Look at these examples, then test yourself on the puzzles. You can find the answers on page 28.

a **short** *cat*
long *plate paid may*
steak weight
prey gauge

e **short** *set dead*
long *eat very demon*
feel sardine
piece ceiling

u **short** *duck come young*
long *clue food prune*
fruit screw do
coupon

o **short** *pop wasp laurel cough*
long *stone soap toe throw*

i **short** *fit syrup build*
long *pie lime sky height*

An eye for an *i*

Only a few words end in *i*. These are mostly from other languages. Can you spell some from the clues below? The first letter of each word is given to help you.

1 Two-piece swimsuit	B	
2 Trip to see animals in the wild	S	
3 Thrown at parades	C	
4 Writing and drawings on public walls	G	
5 Car with driver	T	
6 Long, thin pasta	S	
7 Snow-sport footwear	S	
8 Short skirt	M	
9 Beige-green	K	
10 Type of spicy sausage	S	

Double trouble

Can you guess the half-spelled words in these speech bubbles? Two vowels are missing from each gap.

What b_utiful w_ther!

P_ple confuse us bec_se we're so alike.

I h_rd it'll cl_d over and r_n later tod_.

Your barg_n bl_ j_ns r_lly s_t you.

I've b_n w_ting an h_r for my fr_nd.

I s_d we'd l_ve at the us_l time.

Pl_se can we l_k ar_nd ag_n first?

One vowel short

Which vowel is missing from each of these limericks?

1
There _nce was a man with the n_ti_n,
T_ live _n a b_at _n the _cean,
But his p__r little daughter,
Quite hated the water,
Because _f the up and d_wn m_ti_n.

2
There was an old woman from B_te,
Who played o_t of t_ne on the fl_te,
The noise was so bad
That it drove her q_ite mad
And left her _nable to toot.

3
There once w_s _ brown cow n_med D_isy,
Who w_s pretty but tot_lly l_zy,
She'd gr_ze in her field,
But no milk would she yield,
_nd this drove the f_rmer quite cr_zy.

4
There was a young woman named Lizz_,
Who kept feeling terribl_ dizz_,
She consulted a doctor,
But he onl_ mocked her,
And said that he found it a m_ster_.

5
There was a young g_rl from Tyree,
Who couldn't count further than three,
She tr_ed and she tr_ed -
But _n va_n. "Oh," she cr_ed,
"Four, f_ve, s_x, _s the problem, you see."

6
Th_r_ onc_ was a young boy named Mik_,
Who rod_ a long way on a bik_,
His l_gs got so sor_,
H_ could cycl_ no mor_,
So inst_ad had to g_t off and hik_.

Silent *e*

Some words end in an *e* which you do not pronounce (such as *same*, *concrete* and *arrive*). This silent *e* is important because it gives the vowel that comes before a long sound. For example, if you add a silent *e* to the ends of *hat*, *bit* and *pet*, they become *hate*, *bite* and *Pete*.

1 Take the silent *e* off each word below. Which words have you now spelled? Do these new words have short or long vowel sounds?

use	**note**	**fate**	**spite**	**made**
hope	**rate**	**kite**	**cute**	**ripe**

2 Now add a silent *e* onto these words, and listen how the sound of each one changes.

bar	**rag**	**hug**	**car**	**fir**
sag	**far**	**par**	**wag**	**her**

3 Which vowel is missing from each of these words? Do they have short or long vowel sounds?

Chin_se	**sh_pe**	**wh_te**	**teleph_ne**
conf_se	**al_ne**	**prod_ce**	**al_ve**
supp_se	**compl_te**	**esc_pe**	**h_me**
resc_e	**comb_ne**	**b_the**	**appet_te**
celebr_te	**am_se**	**sev_re**	**supr_me**

Here are some words in which the letter *y* acts as a vowel. First, use a dictionary to check any meanings you aren't sure of. Next, test your spelling by reading, covering, then writing each word.

TIDY	LYRIC	STYLE
GOODBYE	DYNAMITE	TYPICAL
SYSTEM	CYCLE	SATISFY
DRY	EYE	BUTTERFLY
HYSTERICAL	CAPACITY	RHYTHM
LYNCH	SYMMETRY	DYNASTY
MERCY	TYRANNY	NYLON
GYMNASIUM	HYPNOTIZE	APPLY
MYTHOLOGY	NAVY	OCCUPY
CYMBALS	SUPPLY	SYRINGE
PYTHON	READY	SHY
SYMPHONY	TYRANT	DYING
EMERGENCY	HYMN	UNITY
CRYSTAL	LUXURY	RHYME
TYPEWRITER	PRETTY	LYNX
PYRAMID	CENTURY	SYNTHETIC
ANONYMOUS	IDYLLIC	TYCOON

5

The most usual way to make a singular noun (naming word) plural is to add an *s*. For example, *word/words.* But there are some other ways of making plurals which are explained below.

You should NEVER use an apostrophe (') to make a word plural. Apostrophes show the owner of something (such as *my daughter's books*). They also mark missing letters. For example, the *o* in *are not* is replaced by an apostrophe in *aren't.*

ies If a noun ends in *y*, look at the letter before the *y*. If it is a vowel, just add an *s* (as in *monkey/monkeys*). If it is a consonant, change *y* to *i* and add *es* (as in *baby/babies*).

ves To form the plurals of nouns ending in *ff*, add an *s* (as in *cuffs, cliffs*). But for words ending in *f* or *fe*, change the *f* or *fe* to *v* and add *es* (as in *sheaf/sheaves, knife/knives*). Exceptions are: *dwarfs, chiefs, griefs, roofs, proofs, beliefs* and *safes.* Three words can have either spelling: *wharfs/wharves, hoofs/hooves, scarfs/scarves.*

es To make the plural of nouns which end in *ch, sh, s, ss, x* or *z*, simply add *es.* For example, *torches, dishes, buses, kisses, boxes* and *waltzes.*

oes To make the plural of words ending in *o*, add *s* if there is a vowel before the final *o* (as in *zoo*) or if the word is to do with music (such as *solo* and *soprano*). Also add *s* to *disco* and *photo* (*discos, photos*) and names of peoples, such as *Filipinos.* But when there is a consonant before the final *o* (and the words do not fall into the above categories), add *es.* For example, *potatoes.*

Spies in the skies

Two rival organizations have given their secret agents passwords which end in *y*. One organization's passwords can be made plural by adding an *s*, while the passwords of the other change to *ies*. The agents cannot work out who belongs to which organization. Can you help them by sorting out the passwords into two lists?

activity · enemy · dictionary · key · trolley
convoy · ally · valley · display · century
essay · fly · reply · cherry · abbey
TOY · holiday · body · opportunity · GALAXY
bully · factory · party · delay · journey

oes ies ves es oes ies ves es oes ies ves es oes ies

O! What now?

Words which end in o have been replaced in this poem with pictures. Can you spell the plurals of these things?

IF I WERE A MARTIAN AND I LIVED IN OUTER SPACE
I'D LIKE TO VISIT EARTH ONE DAY AND LOOK AROUND THE PLACE
I'D LIKE TO MEET AN   AND VISIT HIS
THEN TRAVEL TO AUSTRALIA TO SEE A
I'D ROAM THE VAST AND GRASSY PLAINS TO FIND THE
AND TREMBLE AT THE BOTTOM OF A FIERY
I'D SUFFER FROM   BITES IN HOT EXOTIC LANDS
AND I'D LEARN TO PLAY   AND I'D MARCH WITH BIG BRASS BANDS
I'D HAVE A LITTLE VEGETABLE PATCH WHERE I COULD DIG AND SOW
THEN WATCH   AND   PLANTS TAKE ROOT AND GROW
AND JUST IN CASE ONE DAY I SHOULD FORGET THE THINGS I'D DONE
I'D BE SURE TO TAKE A   OF EACH AND EVERY ONE
SO WHEN THE TIME CAME TO RETURN TO WORK ON MY SPACE-STATION
I SHOULD ALWAYS HAVE THESE SOUVENIRS OF MY EARTHLY VACATION

F words

In these sentences, words ending in f, fe and ff are singular, but should be plural. Can you spell their plural forms correctly?

1 It took him three puff to blow out the candles on his birthday cake.
2 "Put on scarf , take handkerchief, and behave yourself ," their mother said.
3 The hoof of the galloping horses thundered over the race course.
4 Deciduous trees shed their leaf every year.
5 The team played badly in both half of the match.
6 The thief blew open all the safe and escaped with treasures worth millions.
7 It is said that cats have nine life .
8 The shelf were stacked with loaf of bread of all shapes and sizes.
9 At night in the mountains, they could hear wolf howling.
10 King Henry VIII had six wife.
11 Some very modern cars come with sun roof .

Singularly confused

Words that were originally from other languages often have strange plurals. Do you know how to spell the plurals of the red words in these sentences?

1 I fell asleep on the bus and ended up at the terminus.
2 In the basket of mushrooms I had picked was a poisonous fungus.
3 Another name for a grub that turns into an insect is a larva
4 My birthday cake was a huge, creamy, chocolate gateau
5 I looked at the test and realized we had been taught the wrong syllabus .
6 CO_2 is the chemical formula for carbon dioxide.
7 The worst thing to do in a crisis is panic.
8 People's lives can be changed by the medium of television.

Plural puzzler

There are a few words which have irregular plurals. For example, one *louse* becomes several *lice*. How many other irregular plurals do you know?

Some nouns, such as *sheep*, stay the same in both the singular and plural. How many more words can you think of like this?

7

Most sounds in English can be spelled in more than one way. So choosing the right spelling for a particular word can be confusing.

k The sound "k" as in *kid* is sometimes known as hard *c*. It can be spelled as in **c**at, **k**i**c**k, a**cc**ordion, e**ch**o and grotes**que**.

air The sound "air" can be spelled as in **ch**air, sh**are**, b**ear**, th**ere**, th**eir**, and a**er**ial.

sh "sh" sounds can be spelled as in **s**ure, ru**sh**, op**ti**on, i**ss**ue, so**ci**al, an**xi**ous and **ch**ef.

shun A "shun" sound is mostly spelled as in a**ction**, man**sion**, mi**ssion**, or comple**xion**. But watch out for cu**shion**, fa**shion**, o**cean**, musi**cian** and suspi**cion**.

zhun "zhun" sound is always spelled **sion** (*as in occasion*), except in words which describe nationality. In these words, "zhun" is spelled **sian** (as in *Asian, Malaysian, Polynesian*).

er/uh The ends of many English words aren't stressed, so differences between them can be hard to hear. For example, the final syllables of the words farm**er**, simil**ar**, camer**a** and act**or** just sound like "er" or "uh". The sound "er" also occurs in the middle of words. In these cases, it can be spelled as in s**er**ve, **ear**th, b**ir**d, w**or**d, p**ur**se, j**our**ney or Febru**ary**.

Conquer kicking *k*

Kevin spells all "k" sounds with only the letter *k*. Can you correct his spelling?

Are you an *air*-head?

There are eleven spelling mistakes in this letter. Can you spot them?

I like

Snakes and krokodiles

Hearing my voice eko

Pikniking in the park

Books about shipwreks

Doing magik triks

Klimbing trees

I dislike

Akting in skool plays

Singing in the koir

Losing my train tiket

Stomak-ake

Kornflakes, chiken and brokoli

Kemistry lessons

Dear Gran,

My first time on an ereplane was really exciting - when I'm a millionair I'm going to have my own private jet. My suitcase was bulging - Dad says I'll never have time to where all the clothes and pears of shoes I've brought. But I still managed to forget my hare brush, and Sue's forgotten her teddy bare.

We have a lovely room to shair that looks out on the sea - their are some rair birds to spot along this part of the coast. We're going to a fare tomorrow.

Take cair - we'll see you soon,

Love,

Donna XXXXXXXX

Internet link: For a link to a website where you can find an online lesson and test about confusing word pairs, go to **www.usborne-quicklinks.com**

r air zhun uh k shun er air zhun uh k shun er

Er ...? Uh ...?

Forgetful Rachel has written two lists to help her remember things. But she has forgotten how to spell "er" and "uh" sounds. Which letters are missing?

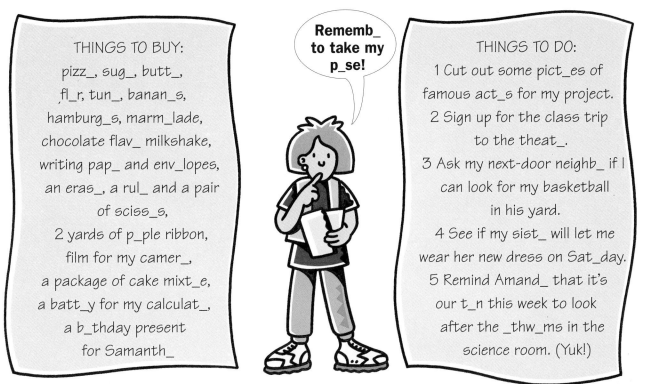

THINGS TO BUY:
pizz_, sug_, butt_,
fl_r, tun_, banan_s,
hamburg_s, marm_lade,
chocolate flav_ milkshake,
writing pap_ and env_lopes,
an eras_, a rul_ and a pair
of sciss_s,
2 yards of p_ple ribbon,
film for my camer_,
a package of cake mixt_e,
a batt_y for my calculat_,
a b_thday present
for Samanth_

Rememb_ to take my p_se!

THINGS TO DO:
1 Cut out some pict_es of famous act_s for my project.
2 Sign up for the class trip to the theat_.
3 Ask my next-door neighb_ if I can look for my basketball in his yard.
4 See if my sist_ will let me wear her new dress on Sat_day.
5 Remind Amand_ that it's our t_n this week to look after the _thw_ms in the science room. (Yuk!)

Be sure of *sh, shun* and *zhun*

Can you complete this newspaper article by spelling a "sh", "shun" or "zhun" sound to replace each numbered gap?

TRAIN CRASH AND CARRY!

There was a colli..1.. at Spellham Station this morning between two express trains. An electri..2.. carried out an investiga..3.. and reported that an explo..4.. had destroyed signals at a junc..5.. down the line. No one was hurt, but in the confu..6.. two bags of ca..7.. were stolen from one of the trains. The police are an..8..ous to solve this crime quickly, and are appealing for informa..9.. . They have i..10..ued a descrip..11.. of two men seen earlier on the platform, who are now under suspi..12.. . One has a musta..13..e and was disguised as a railway offi..14..al. The other had a worried expre..15.. and a bag with the ini..16..als S.H. on it. They both left together in a ..17..auffeur-driven car.

You will almost certainly have seen words spelled with letters that you don't pronounce. These are often letters that used to be pronounced in Old English. For instance, before the 10th century, the *k* in *knot*, the *g* in *gnaw* and the *l* in *folk* were all pronounced. Over the years, the pronunciation of some words changed, while their spellings stayed the same.

So some letters became silent. Other silent letters, such as the *b* in *doubt* and the *p* in *receipt*, were deliberately added during the Renaissance by English scholars. They were trying to make certain words look more like the Latin words they had originally come from.

Here are some common·silent letters, showing when they occur:

b "silent" b sometimes occurs after *m* at the end of a syllable or word (as in *plum**b**er* or *clim**b***). It is also found in *de**b**t, dou**b**t, su**b**tle*.

c can be silent after *s* (as in *s**c**ience* and *s**c**ent*).

k before *n* (as in *k**nife*, ***k**not* and ***k**nitting*).

g often comes before *n* (as in ***g**nome* and *si**g**n*).

h can follow w (as in *w**h**eel*), g (as in *g**h**ostly*), and r (as in *r**h**inoceros*). It is also found at the start of a word (as in ***h**onor*), between vowels (as in *ve**h**icle*), and after x, as in *ex**h**ibit*.

l is sometimes silent before d, k or m (as in *shou**l**d*, *wa**l**k* or *sa**l**mon*).

n can be silent after *m* (as in *hym**n***).

w is sometimes silent in front of *h* (as in ***w**ho*) and also before r at the start of a word (as in ***w**rath* and ***w**reck*).

p is silent before *s, n* or *t* in words which come from Greek (such as ***p**neumatic*). It can also be silent after *s*, as in *ras**p**berry*.

s silent in *i**s**land, i**s**le, ai**s**le*

t is sometimes silent after *s* (as in *fas**t**en*).

Tongue twister teasers

Which silent letter is missing from each of these nonsense tongue twisters?

How quickly can you say each one?

1. We wish we were w_ispering w_ales in w_ite w_irling waters.

2. _nomes, _nats and _nus all _nash and _naw _narled nutshells.

3. Fo_k wa_k cha_ky paths ca_mly sta_king quiet qua_mless sa_mon.

4. The _night who _new the _nack of _nitting _nots _nelt with a _nobbly _napsack on the _noll.

5. The clim_ing plum_er's thum_ grew num_.

6. R_yming, r_ythmical r_inoceroses like r_inestones and r_ubarb.

7. The _retched _riter _reaked his _rath by _renching the _rinkled _rappers from the _recked _ristwatches.

8. Around the solem_ colum_s the singers' hym_s condem_ed the Autum_.

9. G_ostly g_ouls and g_astly g_osts eat g_erkins in g_oulish g_ettos.

Conversation clues

Which silent letters are missing from the words in these speech bubbles?

W..1..at have you been up to?

Last week I had my pa..2..m read by Madame Rippemovsky, the famous ..3..sychic. I was ag..4..ast at the things she ..5..new. She told me all about my "keep the countryside tidy" campai..6..n, also that I don't like lam..7.. chops or egg yo..8..ks, and that ras..9..berries are the fruit I like most. She ..10..new that I want to be a fashion desi..11..ner and that I'd seen an art ex..12..ibition the day before. She told me that I shou..13..d look for my lost s..14..issors in my brown bag, and also that one day I wou..15..d sail on a ya..16..17..t around forei..18..n and exotic i..19..lands with a tall, dark and han..20..some stranger! I hope she's ri..21..22..t!

Hear this

Certain words have letters which some people pronounce, but others don't, such as the *o* in *factory*. See if you can guess a few of them from these clues. The first letter of each is given to help you. Which are the letters that are often silent?

1	Potatoes, carrots, peas...	V
2	The month after January	F
3	A small-scale copy or model	M
4	Another word for precious	V
5	The one after eleventh	T
6	Dark, milk or white	C
7	Fahrenheit or Centigrade	T
8	UK politicians assemble here	P
9	Machine for sucking up dust	V
10	This means out of the ordinary	E
11	Custer was a famous one	G
12	A jewel	D
13	Home for monks	M
14	The day after Tuesday	W

The sound of silence

Can you unscramble the jumbled names of the things pictured here?

There is at least one silent letter in each word. Can you spot them?

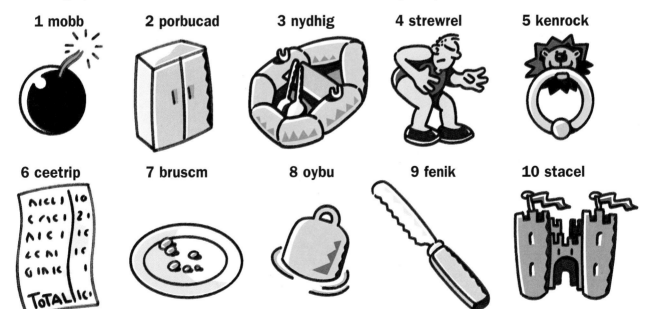

1 mobb
2 porbucad
3 nydhig
4 strewrel
5 kenrock
6 ceetrip
7 bruscm
8 oybu
9 fenik
10 stacel

11

Some letters regularly occur together in combination. But this can be confusing, as one combination of letters can spell different sounds, while a single sound may be spelled by more than one combination.

gh Combinations such as *ough*, *augh*, and *igh* can be tricky, as the *gh* is heard either as "f" (as in *tough*), or is silent (as in *light*). The most difficult is *ough*, as several sounds are spelled this way.

dge A "j" sound at the end of a word or syllable is spelled *ge* if the vowel sound is long (as in *huge*), or when there is a short vowel with a consonant (as in *cringe*). But if there is a short vowel and no consonant, use *dge* (as in *dredge*). An exception to remember is *pigeon*.

qu After the Norman Conquest, French scribes changed the Old English spelling *cw* to *qu*. For example, *cwic* and *cwen* became *quick* and *queen*. Also, in a few words, they spelled a "k" sound with *que*, as in *picturesque*.

tch Watch out for "ch" sounds at the ends of words or syllables. Where there is a short vowel and no consonant, "ch" is spelled *tch*, as in *catch*. The most common exceptions are: *such*, *much*, *attach*, *detach*, *sandwich* and *bachelor*.

Qu quiz

The king can only reach the queen to deliver his bouquet if he can answer these clues correctly. Can you help him? Begin at number one, and find a word that includes *qu* for each clue. The first letter of each word is given in red.

1. OFTEN, OR MANY TIMES F 2. NOT SEE-THROUGH O 3. A SMALL NUT-EATING ANIMAL S 4. TO GIVE IN OR TO GIVE UP Q 5. PEACEFUL OR CALM T 6. WHERE GOLDFISH ARE KEPT A 7. A FOURTH OF SOMETHING Q 8. AN OPEN MINE Q 9. ORIGINAL OR ONE OF A KIND U 10. FOUR-SIDED SHAPE S 11. FAST Q 12. WILLIAM THE ... C 13. WHERE BOATS ARE TIED UP Q 14. AMOUNT Q 15. WASTE MONEY S 16. A WATER-CARRYING BRIDGE A 17. ARGUMENT Q 18. A GROUP OF 4 Q 19. STRANGE Q 20. A KING'S WIFE Q

Do you know what all these *qu* words mean? Test your spelling by reading, covering, then writing each one.

QUADRUPED
LACQUER
ACQUIRE
SQUASH
GROTESQUE
QUOTA
ETIQUETTE
QUALIFICATION
QUINTET
EQUILIBRIUM
QUOTATION
MARQUEE
QUALM
INQUISITIVE
QUILL
ACQUAINTANCE
QUEUE
REQUISITION
QUERY
EQUATION
QUINTESSENTIAL
QUALITY
SQUADRON
REQUEST

ge or *dge*?

The sound "j" is missing from the gaps here. Can you pick the right spelling for each one?

choose *ch* or *tch*

You can complete the article below by replacing each gap with either *ch* or *tch*.

Pet show fiasco

A colle..1.. pet show ended in disaster last week. Besides the usual cats and dogs, some rather stran..2.. entrants emer..3..d, including a he..4..hog, a ba..5..r, and a rock in a ca..6..! The ju..7.. (Annie Mall, a local vet) crin..8..d as a cat ate a mouse called Mi..9..t, and a parrot mana..10..d to fly up to a high le..11.., out of reach. Some people began to fi..12..t, and accused the he..13..hog of having fleas. Its angry owner said that such remarks did dreadful dama..14.. to people's ima..15.. of the creatures, and blows were exchan..16..d. In the confusion, a puppy called Smu..17.. ran off with the ba..18.. for first prize, and was later declared the winner.

Ki..1..en Pun..2..-up!

Guests at a local hotel had only sandwi..3..es for lun..4.. today, as chefs Pierre Noir (Fren..5..) and Jan Van Glyk (Du..6..) were fighting. Noir accused Van Glyk of scor..7..ing his ..8..icken dish by swi..9..ing up the oven. Van Glyk said he hadn't tou..10..ed it and Noir was no ma..11.. for him anyway. The waiters wa..12..ed and ..13..eered as Noir ..14..ased Van Glyk, clu..15..ing a bu..16..er's ha..17..et. Van Glyk threw a ba..18.. of eggs at Noir, who then poured ke..19..up over Van Glyk's head. The enraged Van Glyk pun..20..ed Noir, who fell and hit his head on a ben..21.., while Van Glyk pi..22..ed forward, wren..23..ing his ankle. Both needed to be carried on a stre..24..er to an ambulance. The police fe..25..ed them from the hospital, where Noir received ten sti..26..es, and Van Glyk, a pair of cru..27..es.

The *gh* trap

The combinations *ough*, *augh* and *igh* are missing from these speech bubbles.

But which fits each gap?

Alth_ I like these shoes, they're too h_ and too t_t.

Go thr_ the park and turn r_t. Head for the br_t l_ts.

Come with me. I m_t get lost.

I feel really r_ with this c_ and cold.

I can't help l_ing at the s_t of my n_ty d_ter.

I've had en_ of this bone. It's too t_.

I th_t you were pale.

13

A prefix is a group of letters (such as *inter* or *sub*) which you add onto the beginning of a word to change its meaning. Adding a prefix is quite straightforward - you usually keep all the letters, even if the two you are joining are the same. For example,

dis + satisfied = dissatisfied
un + nerve = unnerve

But when *all* and *well* are used as prefixes, one *l* is dropped. For example, *all* + *ways* = *always*, *well* + *fare* = *welfare*. But do not drop an *l* when *well* is used with a hyphen. For example, *well-made* and *well-off*. On these pages you can test yourself on some of the most common prefixes.

Guesswork

Most prefixes come from Latin, Greek and Old English. Knowing what they mean can often help you guess the meaning of a new word. Can you figure out the meaning of each prefix below by looking at the examples?

trans	transplant	transform	transfusion
re	replace	reunion	recapture
hyper	hypersensitive	hypertension	hyperactive
post	postpone	postnatal	postgraduate
micro	microchip	microwave	microscope
circum	circumference	circumnavigate	circumstance
omni	omnipotent	omnivore	omnibus
auto	autobiography	autopilot	automatic
multi	multinational	multimillionaire	multilateral
photo	photograph	photosynthesis	photosensitive
anti	anticlimax	antifreeze	antihero
pre	prehistoric	prejudge	prepayment
extra	extraterrestrial	extrasensory	extraordinary
mono	monorail	monopoly	monologue

Singled out

Here are some less common prefixes and their meanings:

Do you know what the following words mean?

ante	before/in front of	1	antebellum
ultra	extreme/beyond	2	ultramodern
pseudo	false	3	pseudonym
demi	half	4	demigod
homo	the same/like	5	homophones
intra	inside/within	6	intravenous
mega	large/great	7	megastar
hypo	too little	8	hypothermia
arch	chief	9	archenemy

Picture this

Use the picture clues to guess the prefixes missing from the words below.

1 -pede

2 -scope

3 -circular

4 -natural

5 -happy

6 -cycle

7 -sphere

8 -national

9 -angles

10 -marine

Matching pairs

Can you make words which match the numbered descriptions by joining the prefixes and words below?

1	below freezing	8	above the ground floor
2	junction	9	not to be relied upon
3	below the earth	10	to come back again
4	naughtiness	11	to overcome something
5	not usual	12	action to avoid danger
6	deceitful, lying	13	happening twice a year
7	against the law	14	too many to count

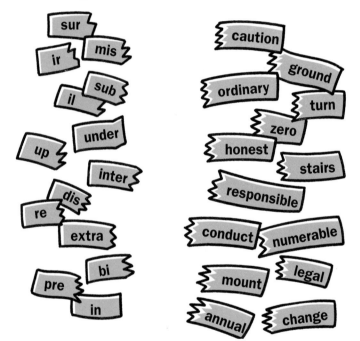

Precise prefixes

Try replacing each of these descriptions with a word that begins with a prefix.

1 lots of different shades
2 to put off until later
3 a self-written life story
4 fluent in two languages
5 an advance showing
6 not cooked enough
7 to vanish
8 to translate a secret message
9 forever
10 to seek out information
11 a disappointing ending
12 not contented
13 unchanging level of sound
14 to change drastically
15 flawed

Face the opposition

Try forming the opposites of the words in capitals below by adding either *un, il, im, mis, in, ir,* or *dis* onto the front of them.

"How dare you OBEY me!" the king shouted.

Cruelty to animals is completely NECESSARY.

Her writing was so bad it was LEGIBLE.

The 16th century vase I had smashed was REPLACEABLE.

Cats have very DEPENDENT natures.

It is very PROBABLE that we will have snow in August.

Drugs are LEGAL in most countries.

Due to our CALCULATIONS, the carpet was the wrong size.

I could see by the scowl on her face that she APPROVED.

At present, it is POSSIBLE for men to have have babies.

"Hurry up! We haven't got all day," she yelled PATIENTLY.

To waste paper is to be environmentally RESPONSIBLE.

We had the FORTUNE to miss each other at the airport.

Although he regretted it, his decision was REVERSIBLE.

In both looks and personality, the twins were SIMILAR.

The MANAGEABLE children ran riot in the classroom.

I used to be DECISIVE, but now I'm not so sure.

It is POLITE to open your mouth while chewing your food.

Soft c

An "s" sound before *i, y* or *e* can be spelled with a soft *c*, as in *con*c*ept,* **c***ylinder* and **c***ircumstan*c*e.* If a word finishes with a long vowel or a consonant followed by an "s" sound, it is often spelled *ce* (as in *tra*c*e* and *innocen*c*e).* This is because *se* at the end of a word usually spells a "z" sound (as in *exercise*).
* Exceptions include *tense, precise, collapse, expense, immense, response, suspense* and *sense.*

Hard g

A "g" as it sounds in *green* is known as hard *g*. In certain words, the letter *u* separates a hard *g* from *e* or *i* (as in *guest* and *guide*). Sometimes *u* also separates a hard *g* and the letter *a* (as in *guarantee, guard* and *language*). Certain words end with a hard *g* spelled *gue* (for example, *fatigue, rogue* and *league*).

Soft g

The sound "j" before *e, i* or *y* can be spelled with a soft *g*, as in **g***entle,* **g***inger* and **g***ymnastics.* At the ends of words, the sound "jee" is spelled *gy* (as in *biology*) and the sound "idj" is spelled *age* (as in *manage*). *Acknowledge, porridge* and *college* are the most common exceptions to remember.

Endings

Here is a rule for adding endings to words which finish in soft *c* or *g* followed by *e* (like *face* and *stage*). Drop the final *e* if the ending starts with a vowel (*stage + ing = staging*), but keep it if the ending starts with a consonant (*face + less = faceless*). But when adding *ous*, keep *e* after soft *g* (*courage + ous = courageous*), and change it to *i* after soft *c* (*grace + ous = gracious*). Also keep the *e* when adding *able* (as in *peace + able = peaceable*).

Get guessing

Meet private investigator Guy Roper. He puts words containing hard *g* sounds into code. Can you crack it?

Did you 7, 21, 5, 19, 19 it was me?
I'm so good at 4, 9, 19, 7, 21, 9, 19, 9, 14, 7 myself that even my 3, 15, 12, 12, 5, 1, 7, 21, 5, 19 don't recognize me. I7, 21, 1, 18, 1, 14, 20, 5, 5 I'll solve any mystery, however 9, 14, 20, 18, 9, 7, 21, 9, 14, 7 it is. If you know where to look, you can always find clues to 7, 21, 9, 4, 5 you to a 7, 21, 9, 12, 20, 25 person.
At the moment, I'm undercover as a musician - that's why I have a 7, 21, 9, 20, 1, 18. But unluckily musical notes are a foreign 12, 1, 14, 7, 21, 1, 7, 5 to me. I have to be on my 7, 21, 1, 18, 4 all the time so I don't blow my cover.
Shhhh! Someone's coming.
I'd better 7, 5, 20 away ...

Putting an end to it

Can you add endings to the words in capitals, so that the sentences read correctly? Make any spelling changes you think are necessary to alter each word correctly.

1 Gandhi was a PEACE man.
2 I'm no good at SLICE cake.
3 Our new house is very SPACE.
4 His suitcase was UNMANAGE.
5 Designer clothes are OUTRAGE expensive.
6 I like hot and SPICE curries.
7 Bright red is very NOTICE.
8 Small oranges are JUICE.
9 He GLANCE around nervously.
10 The bull was CHARGE at me.
11 His JUDGE was too harsh.
12 The stain is SCARCE visible.
13 Tap DANCE is fun.
14 Firefighters are COURAGE.
15 Try BALANCE on one leg.
16 It is ADVANTAGE to speak several languages.

*Turn to pages 26-27 to find out about certain words which end in *ce* when they are nouns, and *se* when they are verbs.

c g c g c g c g c g c g c g c g c g c g c g c g c g c

Do you get the gist?

Use these clues to guess words with a soft *g*. The first letter of each is given for you.

1   The study of the Earth, its climate, and how people live   G
2   An animal with a long neck   G
3   A likeness of something or someone, perhaps in a mirror   I
4   Bacteria which make you ill   G
5   Dull, dismal or dirty   D
6   Where a car is kept overnight   G
7   A line down the left side of paper   M
8   Starting point, or beginning   O

9   You give someone this when you say you're sorry to them   A
10   This is in the air you breathe   O
11   What you might call a person selfish with money   S
12   A very tall person   G
13   Used for binding up injuries   B
14   Fierce, wild or primitive   S
15   A very intelligent person   G
16   Wire enclosure for animals   C

Spell soft *c*

In these three advertisements, words with soft *c* have been jumbled up. Can you unscramble them?

1

Crunch-U-Like

Try our new raceel!

WE GUARANTEE YOU'LL LOVE OUR CIPEER OF
crunchy oats and
ciyuj stuirc fruit chunks
OR YOUR MONEY BACK!

2

MERRIMAN'S CUCSIR

OPENS AT 8PM WITH A
FACEMINTGIN SICNOSROPE
GAZE AT THE
INOSECRIP OF KNIFE THROWERS
THE NICETRATNOONC OF JUGGLERS
THE CRAGE OF TRAPEZE ARTISTS
THE BLANECA OF HIGH-WIRE
WALKERS
GASP IN ECMINXTEET
AS STEVIE STAR SPINS TWO HUNDRED ASCURSE
AND MARVIN THE MARVELOUS STINYCUILC
MAKES A STEEP ACNEST UP A TIGHTROPE
LAUGH AT THE ENEXTCELL CLOWNS!
BE DEEDVICE BY THE WORLD-FAMOUS MAGICIAN
"THE GREAT MYSTERIO"

SEE THE GREATEST SHOW OF THE TUNRYCE!

3

Sample the ceepa
of
Writington Nature Reserve

A brief film show in our mini-minace rotnudesic
the many different sicpees you can see.

Wander around our curralic nature trail
at your own novinecenec.

Don't forget to visit the swannery, where you can
watch gsnecty and parent swans in their natural habitat

WHY NOT STOP FOR REFRESHMENT AT OUR SELF-VEERSIC CAFE?
SEE YOU SOON!

The ends of many English words are not emphasized. This means that differences can be difficult to hear and so also to spell.

able/ible

The endings *able* and *ible* are often confused, as they both sound and mean the same (to be fit or able to). As *able* is much more common, it's easiest to learn which words end in *ible*. But there are some useful tips to remember.

You usually drop silent *e* when adding *able* or *ible*. For example, *use* + *able* = *usable*, *sense* + *ible* = *sensible*. But remember that after soft *c* or *g* there is an *e* before *able* (for example, *pea**ce**able*, *mana**ge**able*), but not before *ible* (*invin**c**ible*, *unintelli**g**ible*). Also watch out for *soluble*, which has neither *a* nor *i*.

cul

Words which end in the sound "cul" are spelled *cal* if they are adjectives (such as *medical* and *practical*), *cle* if they are nouns (such as *circle*), and sometimes also *kle* (as in *tickle* and *fickle*).

ise/ize

You might see some words spelled both *ize* and *ise* (such as *realize /realise*). This is because in the UK both are correct in many cases. In the US, however, *ize* is the usual spelling. But in both countries there are some words which can only be spelled *ise*. These include: *advise, advertise, compromise, despise, devise, disguise, enterprise, exercise, improvise, revise, supervise, surmise, surprise, televise.*

ence/ance

More words end in *ence* or *ent* than *ance* or *ant*. After hard *c* or *g* use *ance/ant* (as in *significance*), but after a soft *c* or *g* use *ence/ent* (as in *negligent*). Watch out for *dependant* - this means a person who is *dependent*, with no *independence*.

---

w*ise* or w*ize*?

The "ize" sounds are missing from these sentences. But how should each one be spelled - *ise* or *ize*?

1 She was so thin I hardly recogn_d her.

2 Exerc_ is good for you.

3 The second edition has been rev_d.

4 The teacher had 30 children to superv_.

5 My friends organ_d a surpr_ party for me.

6 The music store special_s in pianos.

7 Some snakes hypnot_ their prey.

8 The sales assistant pressur_d me into buying it.

9 I won first pr_ in the competition.

10 Our new puppy was advert_d in the newspaper.

11 When the actor forgot his lines, he had to improv_.

12 I like taking part, but I desp_ losing.

13 My big brother critic_s me.

14 I went trick or treating disgu_d as a vampire.

15 My brother custom_d his bicycle.

Probably horrible

Try replacing each numbered gap in this unusual report with either *able* or *ible*.

Last night, I was driving with the roof of my convert..1.. car down, when a strange light became vis..2.. in the sky. It landed in a nearby field, and I set off to investigate. As I drew nearer to the light, a spaceship became recogniz..3.. It wasn't advis..4.. to hang around, but I was unmov..5.. at the terr..6.. sight. Suddenly, a kind of collaps..7.. ladder appeared - whatever horr..8.. things were lurking inside wanted to be soci..9.. I didn't wait to find out if they were peace..10... but ran for my life. It's understand..11.. if you find my incred..12.. story unbeliev..13.. as I have no reli..14.. proof. But I am sens..15... respons..16... and not at all gull..17.. . I never thought life in outer space was poss..18... but this unforgett..19.. experience has made me change my mind.

ul ible cul ize able ul ible cul ize able ul ible cul ize

Possibly problematical

The clues below describe words which end with a "cul" sound. The first letter of each word is given, to help you guess them. How is each word spelled?

1 **What the p stands for in P.E**   P
2 **Round shape**   C
3 **Something in your way**   O
4 **Hanging finger of ice**   I
5 **Vegetables preserved in vinegar**   P
6 **Of utmost importance**   C

7 **Where your foot joins your leg**   A
8 **A type of music**   C
9 **Single eye glass**   M
10 **Cars, trucks etc. are all types of this**   V
11 **Two-wheeled transportation**   B
12 **In the surrounding area**   L

Trail finder

The letters *a* and *e* are missing from the words in this grid. Starting at the top left arrow, there is an invisible path of *ant* and *ance* words through the surrounding *ent* and *ence* words, leading out at the bottom right arrow*. Can you find this path?

acquaint-nce		resid_nce			excell_nt		accid_nt
confid_nce	clear_nce	cli_nt	differ_nce	serv_nt	adjac_nt	inst_nt	sent_nce
differ_nce	allow_nce	evid_nt	griev_nce	appar_nt	import_nt	obedi_nt	fragr_nt
innoc_nt	ignor_nt	refer_nce	defend_nt	circumfer_nce	frequ_nt	pres_nce	reluct_nce
	sil_nt	ramp_nt			interfer_nce	persever_nce	
	occurr_nce	influ_nce	exist_nce	nuis_nce	impertin_nt	appear_nce	
intellig_nt	perman_nt	assist_nt	appli_nce	viol_nt	disturb_nce	promin_nt	consequ_nce
differ_nce	observ_nt	audi_nce	appar_nt	abs_nce	immin_nt	prud_nt	insol_nce
par_nt	dilig_nt	lieuten_nt	attend_nce	ten_nt	resembl_nce	insur_nce	pret_nce
conveni_nt		effici_nt			consci_nce		ambul_nce

Here are some words which end in *ible*. Do you know what they all mean?

Test your spelling by reading, covering, then writing each one.

EXHAUSTIBLE	CONTEMPTIBLE	IRRESISTIBLE	REVERSIBLE
NEGLIGIBLE	IMPERCEPTIBLE	OSTENSIBLE	PERMISSIBLE
INDIGESTIBLE	SUSCEPTIBLE	TANGIBLE	EXTENDIBLE
DISCERNIBLE	FORCIBLE	INDESTRUCTIBLE	ACCESSIBLE
DIVISIBLE	EDIBLE	FLEXIBLE	INDELIBLE
LEGIBLE	PLAUSIBLE	INCORRIGIBLE	FEASIBLE
DISMISSIBLE	ELIGIBLE	ADMISSIBLE	FALLIBLE
REPREHENSIBLE	INCOMPREHENSIBLE	CORRUPTIBLE	DEDUCTIBLE

*The path can lead horizontally, vertically or diagonally.

A suffix is a letter, or combination of letters, added onto the end of a word to change either the meaning or the way the word is used. You usually need to make some alterations in order to add a suffix.

e If a word ends in silent *e*, drop the *e* when adding a suffix which begins with a vowel (for example, *examine* + **ation** = *examination*). But watch out for *age* + *ing*, as both *aging* and *ageing* are correct. Other exceptions include: *acreage, singeing, dyeing, gluey*, words to which *able* is added (such as *loveable*), and words ending in soft *c* or soft *g* when *ous* is added (see page 16).

If the suffix begins with a consonant, keep the *e* (for example, *care* + **less** = *careless*). Exceptions to this include: *argue* + *ment* = *argument, awe* + *ful* = *awful, due* + *ly* = *duly, true* + *ly* = *truly, whole* + *ly* = *wholly*.

ous The suffix *ous* means "full of" (as in *generous* - full of generosity). When adding *ous* to *labor*, you need to add an *i* (*laborious*). Also watch out for words which end in *f*, as this changes to *v* when *ous* is added. For example, *grie**f**/grie**v**ous, mischie**f**/mischie**v**ous*.

y Many people find it confusing to add a suffix to a word ending in *y*. The rule is similar to the one for forming plurals (see page 6). Look at the letter before the *y*. If it is a vowel, just add the suffix. For example, *enjoy* + *ment* = *enjoyment*. If it is a consonant, change the *y* to *i*. For example, *luxury* + *ous* = *luxurious, heavy* + *ness* = *heaviness, plenty* + *ful* = *plentiful*.

But there are several exceptions to remember. Always keep a final *y* when adding *ing*. So *bury* + *ing* = *burying*, but *bury* + *ed* = *buried*. Also keep a final *y* before adding *ish* (as in *babyish*), and whenever the *y* sounds like long "i" (as in *shyly*). When adding the suffix *ous* to *pity, beauty* and *plenty*, you need to change the final *y* to *e*, not *i*, as in *piteous, beauteous* and *plenteous*. Also beware of another two exceptions: *joy* + *ous* = *joyous* and *calamity* + *ous* = *calamitous*. The letter *y* unexpectedly changes to *i* in the following: *lay/laid, pay/paid, say/said, slay/slain, day/daily, gay/gaily/gaiety*.

How about *ous*?

Try forming adjectives ending in *ous* from the nouns in capitals below.

1. Modeling is a GLAMOUR profession.
2. Lightning is extremely DANGER.
3. Japan is a very MOUNTAIN country.
4. I am reading a HUMOR book.
5. Matthew is a STUDY pupil.
6. I am always ANXIETY to arrive on time.
7. Monkeys are MISCHIEF creatures.
8. Housework is dull and LABOR.
9. A dancer's life demands RIGOR discipline.
10. Be CAUTION when crossing the road.

ty ing **ness** y ful e ous ity ing **ness** y ful e ous ity ing

Now you see it...

Sometimes a letter "disappears" when you add a suffix - usually a vowel in the last syllable. For example, tig**e**r + ess = tigress. Try joining the words and suffixes opposite. You will need to make a letter disappear from each one. (Beware of numbers 8 and 10. You need to make an additional change to each of these.)

1 curious + ity
2 hinder + ance
3 repeat + ition
4 exclaim + ation
5 disaster + ous
6 administer + ate
7 four + ty
8 pronounce + ation
9 waiter + ess
10 maintain + ance
11 winter + y
12 explain + ation
13 monster + ous
14 vain + ity
15 remember + ance
16 nine + th

All's well that ends well

Can you add suffixes to the words in pink here, so that this letter makes sense? You will have to decide what to do with the silent e on the end of each word.

Dear Jamal,
I'm WRITE to invite you to my birthday CELEBRATE next Thursday at the AMUSE park. It's still undergoing RENOVATE but will be open from Monday. It'll be very EXCITE. There's an AMAZE water-flume and a really SCARE roller coaster. If you're EXTREME DARE, there's also a huge wheel in which you go backwards and upside down while REVOLVE sideways. Can you IMAGE it? Even I might not be ADVENTURE enough for that! Dad says he'll do the DRIVE, so don't have an ARGUE with your parents about how you're going to get there and back. I was USE at PERSUADE Dad to come in, too. He thinks it'll be TIRE and NOISE. So, we can go on our own as long as we're on our best BEHAVE and act SENSE. Let me know if you're COME. I'm really HOPE to see you. It should be TRUE brilliant.
　　Lots of love,
　　Miles

P.S. I'm sending INVITE to Tanya and Steve too, but it's LIKE Tanya won't come. She's quite NERVE and says you have to be RIDICULE to enjoy being frightened.

What to do with *y*

Follow these paths to find out which word leads to which suffix. Can you join them correctly? How many other ways can you find of joining these words and suffixes?

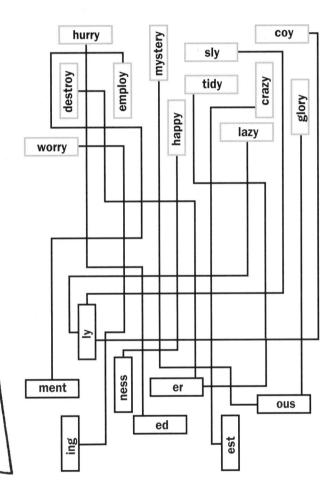

A real hand*ful*

When added as a suffix, *full* is spelled *ful* (as in *helpful*). But the suffix *fully* keeps the double *l* (as in *helpfully*). Here are some more examples:

skillful, spoonfuls, peacefully, beautiful, tasteful, joyfulness, useful, willfully, graceful, forgetfulness. Can you think of any others?

ie/ei Many people have problems spelling words which include *ie* or *ei*. Remembering this rhyme can be helpful:

I BEFORE E EXCEPT AFTER C-
BUT ONLY WHERE THESE LETTERS
SOUND LIKE LONG "E"

For example, the long "e" sound in *believe* is spelled *ie*, but this same sound is spelled *ei* in *perceive* as it occurs after the letter *c*.

There are some exceptions though, the most common of which are *seize*, *weird*, *caffeine*, *species* and *protein*.

But *ie* and *ei* sometimes make sounds other than long "e". For example, *ie* and *ei* can spell a long "i" sound (as in *society* and *height*). *Ei* can also spell a long "a" (as in *weight*), or the sound "air" (as in *their*). Watch out for tricky spellings like these.

---

i and *e* quick quiz

Use the picture clues to help you unscramble these words. Each one contains *ie* or *ei*.

1   ITHEF   **2   HEGIT**   **3   WIVE**   **4   DIFLE**

5   ITE   **6   FRAKEHIDENCH**   **7   DILSHE**   **8   ROSELID**

Here are some words which include ie and ei. Look them up in a dictionary if you don't know what they mean. Next, test your spelling by reading, covering, then writing each one.

SURFEIT	BELIEF	GAIETY	SIEGE
YIELD	EXPERIENCE	SKEIN	FEINT
RECEIPT	FREIGHT	DIESEL	LIEUTENANT
REIGN	CONCEIT	SIEVE	ACQUIESCE
MEDIEVAL	GRIEVANCE	RETRIEVE	BEIGE
LIE	PERCEIVE	SHEIK	CONSCIENCE
TIER	RELIEF	PIERCE	SERIES
EFFICIENT	WEIR	CEILING	THEIR
CONVENIENT	GEISHA	BIER	QUIET
RECIPIENT	MOVIES	ORIENTAL	RELIEVE
ATHEIST	EIDERDOWN	FIEND	ALIEN
SEISMIC	PIETY	SIENNA	DEITY

Missing pieces

Can you finish off these words correctly? They all include *ie* or *ei*.

1   Mrs. Jones and Mrs. Patel are next-door n_.
2   "Pat_ is a virtue," the p_ told his congregation.
3   The E_ Tower is in Paris.
4   Max is a very diso_ dog.
5   Pirates' gold is also known as "p_ of e_".
6   Santa Claus's s_ is drawn by seven r_.
7   When the portrait was unv_, they all saw it had gone!
8   He was h_ to the throne.

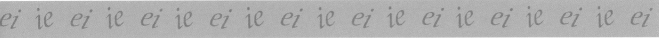

ei ie ei ie ei ie ei ie ei ie ei ie ei ie ei ie ei

Check up on *ie* and *ei*

The following words are missing from "Fierce Justice": *society*, *reprieve*, *chief*, *brief*, *feigned*, *achievement*, *lenient*. Can you choose the right one to replace each numbered gap? Next, see if you can rearrange the jumbled words in "Tips for Tops" to find Dr. Ivor Cure's hints for a healthy life.

Finally, *ie* and *ei* have been left out of the horoscopes below. But which combination completes each word?

Fierce Justice!

BANK ROBBER SENTENCED TO 125 YEARS

A judge has sentenced two men accused of robbing a bank at gunpoint to 125 years in prison. Throughout their ..1.. trial the men ..2.. innocence, in the hope of a ..3.. But the judge said he could not be ..4.. as the pair were obviously a menace to ..5.. . ..6.. Inspector Lawless said that putting these bad criminals behind bars was a great ..7.. .

TIPS FOR TOPS

1 Make sure your **tide** contains plenty of **tirpone**.
2 Watch your **thewig**.
3 Reduce your cholesterol intake - it's bad for your **seniv**.
4 Drink **dacefatfendie** coffee.
5 Eat a **yearvit** of foods, to make sure you get all the **sunnitret** necessary for good health.
6 Spend some of your **reelius** time each week exercising.
7 Meditate regularly, in order to **reeveil** stress and **texyain**.
8 Make sure you have a bath or shower every day. Personal **heegyin** is very important.

Star spot

Aquarius
You will rec..1..ve a gift.

Pisces
Don't get too t..2..d up with people's problems.

Aries
Have a night out with fr..3..nds.

Taurus
Watch out for counterf..4..t money.

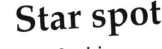
Gemini
The results of a sc..5..ntific experiment will interest you.

Cancer
You will take ..6..ther a boat or plane trip.

Leo
Make a recipe using unusual ingred..7..nts.

Virgo
Don't let a stranger dec..8..ve you.

Libra
S..9..ze the chance for a new exper..10..nce.

Scorpio
It's a good time to begin learning a for..11..gn language.

Sagittarius
Visit some anc..12..nt ruins.

Capricorn
You will hear from a distant relation, perhaps a nephew or n..13..ce.

23

Words with double letters (such as nece*ss*ary) are confusing to spell. But knowing whether to double a final letter when adding a suffix is even more difficult. It depends on the number of syllables in a word and where the stress lies. There are also special rules for words ending in *r* and *fer*.

one When adding a suffix to a word of one syllable, a short vowel sound and one final consonant* you do not normally double the final letter. For example *worship/worshiped/ worshiping*. Watch out for exceptions to this rule such as *gladden, woolly* and *crueller*. If you are unsure, check in a dictionary.

fer In two-syllable words which end in *fer*, the stress sometimes changes from the final syllable to the first syllable when a suffix is added. In these cases, do not double the final *r*. For example, *re**fer** +ee = **refer**ee*, *pre**fer** +able =**prefer**able*. When the stress does not change place, use the rule for words ending in *r*. For example, *re**fer** + ing = re**ferr**ing*.

r A final *r* stays single if the stress is on the first syllable (for example, *offer/offering*). If the stress is on the second syllable, double the *r* (for example, *oc**cur**/oc**curr**ing*). But if there are two vowels before the *r*, leave it single (as in *desp**air**/desp**air**ing*).

two For two-syllable words which end in one consonant* (such as *pilo**t***), don't double the final letter if the stress falls on the first syllable (for example, *pilot + ing = piloting, gallop + ed = galloped*). When the stress lies on the second syllable, double the final letter if the suffix begins with a vowel, but leave it single if it begins with a consonant. For example, *re**gret** + ing = re**grett**ing*, but *re**gret** + fully = re**gret**fully*.

Missing doubles

Double *b, c, d, f, g, l, m, n, p, r, s, t* and *z* are missing from the pages of this story. But which do you need to complete each word?

I had had a fu..1..y feeling about things from the begi..2..ing. I had mi..3..ed my co..4..ection - the last train till morning, so asked someone (a sma..5.. man with a shifty a..6..earance and a nervous ma..7..er) to reco..8..end a hotel. Leaving my lu..9..age, I set off. The weather was ho..10..ible - to..11..ential rain poured down my co..12..ar and co..13..ected in my boots, while the wind whi..14..ed around me. After walking for ages down a deserted road, with no sign of any a..15..o..16..dation, I was ge..17..ing i..18..itable and depre..19..ed. Su..20..enly, I saw da..21..ling headlights coming from the o..22..osite direction. I a..23..empted to a..24..ract the driver's a..25..ention, but the car a..26..elerated as it a..27..roached! I leapt out of the way, just avoiding a co..28..ision, and ho..29..led to the side of the road. Having na..30..owly avoided a te..31..ible a..32..ident, I was also u..33..erly lost. What was I to do? Just then, I noticed a light in the distance. I trudged towards it through the su..34..ounding darkne..35.., over pe..36..les and through pu..37..les of mu..38..y water, until eventua..39..y

I a..40..ived at a sha..41..y li..42..le co..43..age. I knocked, cautiously, but there was no reply. Su..44..re..45..ing my nerves, I heaved the door open with a great e..46..ort, and ste..47..ed into a dark pa..48..age. On my i..49..ediate right stairs led down - I a..50..ume to the ce..51..ar. An o..52..ensive sme..53.. came wafting up. In a room to my left, a table was set with food and a cup of co..54..ee - still warm. I was pu..55..led as to why the o..56..upant had left in such a hu..57..y. But before I could satisfy my a..58..etite by a..59..acking the food, I realized with a shu..60..er that I was not alone! I turned around to find myself looking down the ba..61..el of a gun. A man with a ha..62..ard expre..63..ion was calmly si..64..ing by the door, behind me. I hoped he didn't have an itchy tri..65..er finger . I could tell he was a profe..66..ional vi..67..ain by the way he said, "Don't make it nece..68..ary for me to shoot you." I didn't like his a..69..itude one bit. But as my mo..70,.o is "never say die," I determined to try to escape at the first o..71..ortunity, or find a way to get a me..72..age to someone, somehow.

*When a word ends with two consonants, the final letter always stays single. For example, *star**t** + ed = started*, *preven**t** + ing = preventing*.

gg rr zz ll bb ll gg rr zz ll bb ll gg rr zz ll bb ll

Watch out for the double letters in these words:

ACCURATE
VACCINATE
PROFESSION
IRRITATE
DESICCATE
SUGGEST
POSSESS
AGGRESSION
EMBARRASS
ADDRESS
INFLAMMABLE
DISSECT
APPLAUSE
ACCURATE
CORRESPOND
NECESSARY
ERROR
ASSESS
COMMAND
QUESTIONNAIRE
COMMUNICATION
EXAGGERATE
INTERRUPT
DISAPPOINT
ECCENTRIC
INTERROGATE
SUCCEED
PARALLEL

Doubling decisions

Here is an interview with Bob Barley, singer with The Howlers. To make it read correctly, try adding an ending to each word in capitals. But watch out for any letters that need to be doubled.

Q How did you become a star?
A I can DIM remember asking for a guitar when I was three. I SHOW that I was REAL talented as soon as I START playing.

Q Have you had any setbacks?
A In the BEGIN things moved SLOW and I had HARD any money. But FAIL never CROSS my mind. I GRAB the chance of RECORD my first single, "I'm FALL for you babe", and I never LOOK back.

Q What do you like best about your job?
A TRAVEL the world and SING live. HEAR the crowd CHEER at the OPEN of a concert is the GREAT FEEL in the world, man.

Q How do you like to spend Sunday?
A STAY in bed and FLIP through the newspapers while SIP a cup of coffee.

Q What's the worst aspect of being famous?
A Being SPOT by fans and MOB wherever I go.

Q Do you ever think of QUIT the business?
A As I get OLD, I do think about STEP down and LET the youngsters take over. But although my hair's GET THIN, I'm not giving up yet.

Q When can we expect a new album from The Howlers?
A We've just SCRAP our latest material to try a change of direction. We're JAM in the studio at the moment.

Q What's your DEEP fear?
A DROP out of the charts and my fans FORGET me.

Q What are your REMAIN aims?
A I want to be an even BIG star!

Problem patterns

Here are some difficult spelling patterns. Look at the base word, then decide whether the missing consonants should be single or double in the words which follow.

1	deter	dete_ed	7	common	commo_er	12	cruel	crue_er
		dete_ing			commo_est			crue_est
		dete_ent			commo_ess			crue_y
2	fit	fi_est	8	bat	ba_er			crue_ty
		fi_ing			ba_ed	13	star	sta_dom
		fi_fully			ba_ing			sta_ed
3	open	ope_er	9	forget	forge_able			sta_ing
		ope_ing			forge_ing	14	commission	commissio_er
		ope_ess			forge_ful			commissio_ing
4	model	mode_ed	10	commit	commi_ee	15	defer	defe_ed
		mode_ing			commi_ing			defe_ing
5	occasion	occasio_al			commi_ment			defe_ment
		occasio_ally	11	occur	occu_ed			defe_able
6	hop	ho_ed			occu_ing	16	happen	happe_ing
		ho_ing			occu_ence			happe_ed

25

Here are some especially difficult tests. If you can answer all these correctly, you can be sure that you are an excellent speller!

c or s?

A few words are spelled with *c* when they are nouns, but with *s* when verbs. For example, *advice* and *advise*, *device* and *devise*, *prophecy* and *prophesy*. Notice how the pronunciation changes slightly with the spelling. This will help you choose the correct spelling for the way the word is being used.

there/there's/their/theirs/they're

These spellings are very often confused. *There* is the opposite of *here*. *Their* and *theirs* show ownership (for example, *their books*, and *the books are theirs*). *They're* is short for *they are*. *There's* can mean two things: it is usually short for *there is*, but when followed by *been*, it is a short form of *there has*.

Homophones

Homophones are words which sound the same, but which have different spellings and meanings. For example, *there*, *their* and *they're*; *no* and *know*; *past* and *passed*; *threw* and *through*.

Watch out for words which have an "f" sound spelled *ph*. Here are some for you to test yourself on.

PHASE
ORPHAN
PHOBIA
GRAPH
CENOTAPH
PHYSIQUE
EPITAPH
SPHERE
ELEPHANT
PHONOGRAM
PHANTOM
NEPHEW
MICROPHONE
NYMPH
PHRASE
PARAGRAPH
PHEASANT
PHLEGM
CATASTROPHE
METAPHOR
PAMPHLET
PARAPHERNALIA
APOSTROPHE
PHARMACY
PHENOMENON
PHYSIOTHERAPY
DIAPHRAGM

Can you do better?

Here is Ike Canspellit's report card. His teachers have made a lot of spelling mistakes - can you spot them all?

Name Ike Canspellit **Class** Upper 4

Subject	Comments	Grade
SPORTS	Ike is skillfull on the football feeld and in the swiming pool.	B+
MUSIC	More self-disiplin and practice are neccesary, but Ike has a good scents of rithum.	C
DRAMA	IKE INJOYS BOTH TRADGEDY AND COMIDY AND IS A TALENTED CARACTER ACTER.	B
MATH	Ike has benifitted from atending extra classes. He has definitely improoved, but still makes fawlts threw carelesness	C
JOGRAPHY	Ike's prodject on equitorial rain forrest's was very nollidgible.	B-
SCIENCE	Ike is unintrested in sience and looses consentration easily. He also displays a tendancy to talk. During practicle work in the laboratry he medals with the ecqipment. His techneeks are very disapointing.	D
HISTRY	Ike has a thurugh under standing of the Ainshent World, espeshally of the lifes of the Roman emporers. He has enjoyed lerning about the gods and godeses of Greek mitholojee.	A-
INGLISH	Altho Ike makes littel errers in his grammer, his creativ riting is genrally exsellent. His discriptions are perseptive and ofen humorus. We have been greatful for his asistence in the libry this year. As usuall, Ike is top of the class at spelling.	A+

Signature Ms V. Unfriendly **Date** July 1st

Internet link: For a link to a website where you can learn new words, find antonyms, synonyms and watch mini animations that explain their meanings, go to www.usborne-quicklinks.com

s *their* c *there* s *their* c *there* s *their* c *there* s *their*

Noun or verb?

Try replacing each of the gaps in these sentences with either *c* or *s*. In order to pick the right spelling, you need to decide whether each word with a missing letter is a noun or a verb.

1 **He had devi_ed a cunning plan.**
2 **I advi_ed her not to give up trying.**
3 **Whoever devi_ed the alarm clock was very clever. It is a useful devi_e.**
4 **A clairvoyant prophe_ied my future, but I will be very surprised if her prophe_y comes true.**
5 **She took absolutely no notice of my excellent advi_e.**

Sound-alike

Can you pick the correct spellings from the homophones on this page of Wendy's diary?

5th April

The weather/whether today was fowl/foul, but I'd promised to meat/meet Grandad at half passed/past two/to/too. He was already/all ready there. He waived/waved when he saw/sore me. He said he'd only had a short wait/weight. He asked if I'd mist/missed him - of course/coarse! It was poring/pouring with rain, but we wandered/wondered along the beach/beech anyway. He said I'd groan/grown since he'd last scene/seen me - what a complement/compliment! I said he should try dyeing/dying his white hair/hare. He laughed, and tolled/told me that he hated the whole/hole business of

Saturday

getting old. He said it seemed only yesterday when he used to read bedtime stories/storeys aloud /allowed to me. We talked about how board/bored I am at school. Grandad said I should no/know that every lessen/lesson is important, and that my opinion will alter/altar. That maybe/may be sow/so/sew, but I'm shore/sure I'll never enjoy chemistry! I led/lead the way to the station to ensure/insure that he didn't get lost. He asked me to right/write soon, and gave me some stationery/stationary with my name and address at the top of every peace/piece of paper.

Can you get *there*?

Can you think of shorter ways to say the underlined parts of these sentences?

You will have to use *there*, *there's*, *their*, t*heirs*, or *they're* in each one.

1 **Look! There is Michelle!**
2 **Look at that, over in that direction!**
3 **I know they are going away today.**
4 **The house belonging to them is huge.**
5 **I want one just like the one they have.**
6 **There has been a dreadful accident.**

7 **Drop it! It's the one belonging to them.**
8 **There has been a snowfall overnight.**
9 **I liked the friends belonging to them.**
10 **Have some more. There is plenty left.**
11 **I hate going to that place.**
12 **They are always arguing.**

The final frontier

Here are just a few of the most commonly misspelled words. Why not make your own list of difficult spellings?

ACCOMMODATION
ACKNOWLEDGE
AERIAL
ALCOHOL
ALTOGETHER
AMATEUR
ANNIHILATE
APARTMENT
AWKWARD

BACHELOR
BANKRUPTCY
BEAUTIFUL
BUSINESS

CALIBER
CALENDAR
CAMOUFLAGE
CARICATURE
CEMETERY
COLONEL
CONSCIOUS
CRITICISM

DECREPIT
DESCENDANT
DISSUADE

ENVIRONMENT
EXERCISE
EXHAUST

FLUORESCENT
FOREIGNER

GASES
GAUGE
GUARANTEE

IDYLLIC
INDISPENSABLE
INSTALLMENT

LIAISON
LIQUEFIED

MEDIEVAL
OCCASION
OPPORTUNITY

PECULIAR
PERSEVERANCE
POSSESSION
PREJUDICE
PURSUE
PRIVILEGE

QUESTIONNAIRE

RECOMMEND
RHYME

SECRETARY
SEPARATE
SILHOUETTE
SURPRISE

VACUUM
VEHICLE
VICIOUS

27

Page 3

What are syllables?

one syllable:	soap, bread, milk, eggs, cheese
two syllables:	tooth/paste, pea/nuts, cof/fee, hon/ey, on/ions
three syllables:	de/ter/gent, lem/on/ade, to/ma/toes, ba/na/nas, or/an/ges
four syllables:	mac/a/ro/ni, cau/li/flow/er

What is stress?

tooth/paste, *pea*/nuts, *hon*/ey, *cof*/fee, *on*/ions, de/*ter*/gent, lem/on/*ade*, to/*ma*/toes, ba/*na*/nas, *or*/an/ges, mac/a/*ro*/ni, *cau*/li/flow/er

Pages 4-5

An eye for an i

1 bikini   3 confetti   5 taxi   7 ski   9 khaki
2 safari   4 graffiti   6 spaghetti   8 mini   10 salami

Double trouble

What beautiful weather!

People confuse us because we're so alike.

I heard it'll cloud over and rain later today.

Your bargain blue jeans really suit you.

I've been waiting an hour for my friend.

I said we'd leave at the usual time.

Please can we look around again first?

One vowel short

1 *o* is the missing vowel   4 *y* is the missing vowel
2 *u* is the missing vowel   5 *i* is the missing vowel
3 *a* is the missing vowel   6 *e* is the missing vowel

Silent e

1 The new words are: us, not, fat, spit, mad, hop, rat, kit, cut, rip
These all have short vowel sounds.
2 The new words are: bare, rage, huge, care, fire, sage, fare, pare, wage, here
3 The completed words are: Chinese, shape, white, telephone, confuse, alone, produce, alive, suppose, complete, escape, home, rescue, combine, bathe, appetite, celebrate, amuse, severe, supreme
These vowels all have long sounds because of the silent *e* on the end of each word.

Pages 6-7

Spies in the skies

the *ys* organization: convoys, essays, toys, holidays, valleys, keys, displays, delays, trolleys, abbeys, journeys

the *ies* organization: activities, bullies, enemies, allies, flies, factories, dictionaries, replies, bodies, parties, cherries, opportunities, centuries, galaxies

O! What now?

Eskimo/Eskimo**s**	mosquito/mosquito**es**
igloo/igloo**s**	piano/piano**s**
kangaroo/kangaroo**s**	potato/potato**es**
buffalo/buffalo**es**	tomato/tomato**es**
volcano/volcano**es**	photo/photo**s**

Singularly confused

1 termini   4 gateaux   6 formulae
2 fungi   5 syllabi or   7 crises
3 larvae   syllabuses   8 media

F words

1 puff**s**
2 scarf**s** or scar**ves**, handkerchief**s**, yoursel**ves**
3 hoof**s** or hoo**ves**
4 lea**ves**
5 hal**ves**
6 thie**ves**, safe**s**
7 li**ves**
8 shel**ves**, loa**ves**
9 wol**ves**
10 wi**ves**
11 roof**s**

Plural puzzler

Irregular plurals include: *mice, men, women, geese, children, teeth, feet*
Words that are the same in both the singular and the plural include: *deer, salmon, trout, grouse, moose, news, pants, tights, trousers, scissors, fish, mathematics, series, species, innings*

Pages 8-9

Conquer kicking k

Kevin likes:
sna**k**es and **c**rocodiles
hearing his voice e**ch**o
pi**c**ni**ck**ing in the par**k**
boo**k**s about shipwre**ck**s
doing magi**c** tri**ck**s
climbing trees
Kevin dislikes:
a**c**ting in s**ch**ool plays
singing in the **ch**oir
losing his train ti**ck**et
stoma**ch**a**ch**e
cornfla**k**es, **ch**i**ck**en
and bro**cc**oli
chemistry lessons

Er...? Uh...?

THINGS TO BUY:
pizza, sugar, butter, flour, tuna, bananas, hamburgers, marmalade, chocolate flavor milkshake, writing paper and envelopes, an eraser, a ruler and a pair of scissors.
2 yards of purple ribbon, film for my camera, a packet of cake mixture, a battery for my calculator, a birthday present for Samantha

Remember to take my purse!

Are you an air-head?

Dear Gran,

My first time on an **air**plane was really exciting - when I'm a million**air**e I'm going to have my own private jet. My suitcase was bulging - Dad says I'll never have time to w**ear** all the clothes and pairs of shoes I've brought. But I still managed to forget my h**air** brush, and Sue's forgotten her teddy b**ear**.

We have a lovely room to sh**are** that looks out on the sea - there are some r**are** birds to spot along this part of the coast. We're going to a f**air** tomorrow.

Take c**are** - we'll see you soon.

Love,
Donna XXXXXXXX

THINGS TO DO:
1 Cut out some pictures of famous actors for my project.
2 Sign up for the class trip to the theater.
3 Ask my next-door neighbor if I can look for my basketball in his garden.
4 See if my sister will let me wear her new dress on Saturday.
5 Remind Amanda that it's our turn this week to look after the earthworms in the science room. (Yuk!)

Be sure of sh, shun and zhun

1 colli**sion**	7 ca**sh**	13 musta**che**
2 electri**cian**	8 an**xious**	14 offi**cial**
3 investiga**tion**	9 informa**tion**	15 expre**ssion**
4 explo**sion**	10 i**ss**ued	16 initi**als**
5 junc**tion**	11 descrip**tion**	17 **ch**auffeur
6 confu**sion**	12 suspi**cion**	

the gh trap

Although I like these shoes, they're too hi**gh** and too ti**ght**.

I've had enou**gh** of this bone. It's too tou**gh**.

Go throu**gh** the park and turn ri**ght**. Head for the bri**ght** li**ght**s.

Come with me. I mi**ght** get lost.

I feel really rou**gh** with this cou**gh** and cold.

I thou**ght** you were pale.

I can't help lau**gh**ing at the si**ght** of my nau**gh**ty dau**gh**ter.

==== **Pages 10-11** ====

Tongue twister teasers

1 h 2 g 3 l 4 k 5 b 6 h 7 w 8 n 9 h

Conversation clues

1 w**h**at	8 yol**k**	15 woul**d**
2 pal**m**	9 ras**p**berries	16/17 ya**ch**t
3 **p**sychic	10 **k**new	18 forei**gn**
4 ag**h**ast	11 desi**gn**er	19 is**l**ands
5 **k**new	12 exhi**b**ition	20 hand**s**ome
6 campai**gn**	13 shoul**d**	21/22 ri**gh**t
7 lam**b**	14 s**c**issors	

Hear this

1 veg**e**table	6 choc**o**late	11 gen**e**ral
2 Febr**u**ary	7 temp**er**ature	12 di**a**mond
3 mini**a**ture	8 parli**a**ment	13 monast**e**ry
4 valu**a**ble	9 vacu**u**m	14 Wedn**e**sday
5 twelf**th**	10 extr**a**ordinary	

The sound of silence

1 bom**b**	5 **k**nocker	9 **k**nife
2 cu**p**board	6 recei**p**t	10 cas**t**le
3 ding**h**y	7 crum**b**s	
4 **w**restler	8 b**u**oy	

==== **Pages 12-13** ====

Qu quiz

1 fre**qu**ent	8 **qu**arry	15 s**qu**ander
2 opa**que**	9 uni**que**	16 a**qu**educt
3 s**qu**irrel	10 s**qu**are	17 **qu**arrel
4 **qu**it	11 **qu**ick	18 **qu**artet
5 tran**qu**il	12 con**qu**eror	19 **qu**eer
6 a**qu**arium	13 **qu**ay	20 **qu**een
7 **qu**arter	14 **qu**antity	

ge or dge?

1 colle**ge**	7 ju**dge**	13 he**dge**hog
2 stran**ge**	8 crin**ge**d	14 dama**ge**
3 emer**ge**d	9 Mi**dge**t	15 ima**ge**
4 he**dge**hog	10 mana**ge**d	16 exchan**ge**d
5 ba**dge**r	11 le**dge**	17 Smu**dge**
6 ca**ge**	12 fi**dge**t	18 ba**dge**

Choose ch or tch

1 Kit**ch**en	10 tou**ch**ed	19 ket**ch**up
2 Pun**ch**-up	11 ma**tch**	20 pun**ch**ed
3 sandwi**ch**es	12 wat**ch**ed	21 ben**ch**
4 lun**ch**	13 **ch**eered	22 pit**ch**ed
5 Fren**ch**	14 **ch**ased	23 wren**ch**ing
6 Dut**ch**	15 clut**ch**ing	24 stret**ch**er
7 scor**ch**ing	16 but**ch**er's	25 fet**ch**ed
8 **ch**icken	17 hat**ch**et	26 sti**tch**es
9 swit**ch**ing	18 ba**tch**	27 crut**ch**es

==== **Pages 14-15** ====

Guesswork

trans	across/beyond	auto	self
re	again	multi	many/much
hyper	too much	photo	light
post	after	anti	against/opposing
micro	very small	pre	before
circum	around	extra	beyond/outside
omni	all	mono	single

Singled out

1 antebellum - before the Civil War
2 ultramodern - extremely modern
3 pseudonym - a false name, such as used by an author
4 demigod - a half-human, half-immortal being
5 homophones - words which sound the same
6 intravenous - within a vein
7 megastar - a very famous personality
8 hypothermia - abnormally low body temperature
9 arch enemy - chief enemy

Picture this

1 centi	3 semi	5 un	7 hemi	9 tri
2 tele	4 super	6 bi	8 inter	10 sub

Matching pairs

1 subzero	6 dishonest	11 surmount
2 interchange	7 illegal	12 precaution
3 underground	8 upstairs	13 biannual
4 misconduct	9 irresponsible	14 innumerable
5 extraordinary	10 return	

Precise prefixes

1 multicolored	6 underdone	11 anticlimax
2 postpone	7 disappear	12 dissatisfied
3 autobiography	8 decode	13 monotone
4 bilingual	9 always	14 transform
5 preview	10 research	15 imperfect

Face the opposition

disobey, unnecessary, illegible, irreplaceable, independent, improbable, illegal, miscalculations, disapproved, impossible, impatiently, irresponsible, misfortune, irreversible, dissimilar, unmanageable, indecisive, impolite

Pages 16-17

Get guessing

Did you **guess** it was me?
I'm so good at **disguising** myself that even my **colleagues** don't recognize me. I **guarantee** I'll solve any mystery, however **intriguing** it is. If you know where to look, you can always find clues to **guide** you to a **guilty** person.
At the moment, I'm undercover as a musician - that's why I have a **guitar**. But unluckily, musical notes are a foreign **language** to me. I have to be on my **guard** all the time so I don't blow my cover.
Shhhh! Someone's coming.
I'd better **get** away...

Putting an end to it

1	peaceable or peaceful	9	glanced
2	slicing	10	charging
3	spacious	11	judgement or judgment
4	unmanageable	12	scarcely
5	outrageously	13	dancing
6	spicy	14	courageous
7	noticeable	15	balancing
8	juicy	16	advantageous

Do you get the gist?

1	geography	7	margin	13	bandage
2	giraffe	8	origin	14	savage
3	image	9	apology	15	genius
4	germs	10	oxygen	16	cage
5	dingy	11	stingy		
6	garage	12	giant		

Spell soft c

1 Crunch-U-Like. Try our new **cereal**!
We guarantee you'll love our **recipe** of crunchy oats and **juicy citrus** fruit chunks or your money back.

2 Merriman's **Circus** opens at 8pm with a **magnificent procession**.
Gaze at the **precision** of knife throwers, the **concentration** of jugglers, the **grace** of trapeze artists, the **balance** of high-wire walkers.
Gasp in **excitement** as Stevie Star spins two hundred **saucers** and Marvin the Marvelous **unicyclist** makes a steep **ascent** up a tightrope.
Laugh at the **excellent** clowns!
Be **deceived** by the world-famous magician "the Great Mysterio".
See the greatest show of the **century**.

3 Sample the **peace** of Writington Nature Reserve.
A brief film show in our mini-**cinema introduces** the many different **species** you can see.
Wander around our **circular** nature trail at your own **convenience**.
Don't forget to visit the swannery where you can watch **cygnets** and parent swans in their natural habitat.
Why not stop for refreshment at our self-**service** café? See you soon!

Pages 18-19

w*ise* or w*ize*?

1	recognized	6	specializes	11	improvise
2	exercise	7	hypnotize	12	despise
3	revised	8	pressurized	13	criticizes
4	supervise	9	prize	14	disguised
5	organized/ surprise	10	advertised	15	customized

Probably horrible

1	convert**ible**	8	horr**ible**	15	sens**ible**
2	vis**ible**	9	soci**able**	16	respons**ible**
3	recogniz**able**	10	peace**able**	17	gull**ible**
4	advis**able**	11	understand**able**	18	poss**ible**
5	unmov**able**	12	incred**ible**	19	unforgett**able**
6	terr**ible**	13	unbeliev**able**		
7	collaps**ible**	14	reli**able**		

Possibly problematical

1	physi**cal**	5	pi**ckle**	9	mono**cle**
2	cir**cle**	6	criti**cal**	10	vehi**cle**
3	obsta**cle**	7	an**kle**	11	bicy**cle**
4	ici**cle**	8	classi**cal**	12	lo**cal**

Trail finder

The letter *a* is missing from: acquaintance, clearance, allowance, ignorant, rampant, defendant, grievance, servant, important, instant, fragrant, reluctance, perseverance, appearance, disturbance, nuisance, appliance, assistant, observant, lieutenant, attendance, tenant, resemblance, insurance, ambulance. The letter *e* is missing from all the other words in the grid. The path looks like this:

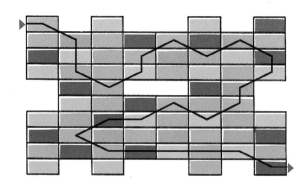

Pages 20-21

How about *ous*?

1	glamorous	5	studious	9	rigorous
2	dangerous	6	anxious	10	cautious
3	mountainous	7	mischievous		
4	humorous	8	laborious		

Now you see it...

1	curiosity	7	forty	13	monstrous
2	hindrance	8	pronunciation	14	vanity
3	repetition	9	waitress	15	remembrance
4	exclamation	10	maintenance	16	ninth
5	disastrous	11	wintry		
6	administrate	12	explanation		

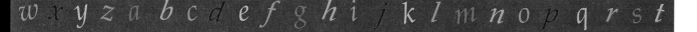

All's well that ends well

writing, celebration, amusement, renovation, exciting, amazing, scary, extremely, daring, revolving, imagine, adventurous, driving, argument, useless, persuading, tiring, noisy, behaviour, sensibly, coming, hoping, truly, invitations, likely, nervous, ridiculous

What to do with *y*

worry + ing = worrying
destroy + er = destroyer
hurry + ed = hurried
employ + ment = employment
mystery + ous = mysterious
happy + ness = happiness

sly + ly = slyly
tidy + er = tidier
lazy + ly = lazily
crazy + est = craziest
coy + ly = coyly
glory + ous = glorious

More combinations: worrier, worried, destroying, destroyed, hurrying, hurriedly, employer, employing, employed, mysteriously, happier, happiest, happily, tidily, tidying, tidiest, tidied, tidiness, slyness, slyest, crazier, crazily, craziness, crazied, lazier, laziest, laziness, glorying, gloried, coyness

Pages 22-23

i and *e* quick quiz

1	thief	4	field	7	shield
2	eight	5	tie	8	soldier
3	view	6	handkerchief		

Missing pieces

1 neighbours
2 patience priest
3 Eiffel
4 disobedient
5 pieces of eight
6 sleigh, reindeer
7 unveiled
8 heir

Fierce Justice

1	brief	4	lenient	7	achievement
2	feigned	5	society		
3	reprieve	6	chief		

Tips for Tops

1 protein
2 weight
3 veins
4 decaffeinated
5 variety, nutrients
6 leisure
7 relieve, anxiety
8 hygiene

Star Spot

1	receive	6	either	11	foreign
2	tied	7	ingredients	12	ancient
3	friends	8	deceive	13	niece
4	counterfeit	9	seize		
5	scientific	10	experience		

Pages 24-25

Missing doubles

1 funny
2 beginning
3 missed
4 connection
5 small
6 appearance
7 manner
8 recommend
9 luggage
10 horrible
11 torrential
12 collar
13 collected
14 whipped
15/16 accommodation
17 getting
18 irritable
19 depressed
20 suddenly
21 dazzling
22 opposite
23 attempted
24 attract

25	attention	41	shabby	57 hurry
26	accelerated	42	little	58 appetite
27	approached	43	cottage	59 attacking
28	collision	44/45		60 shudder
29	hobbled	suppressing		61 barrel
30	narrowly	46	effort	62 haggard
31	terrible	47	stepped	63 expression
32	accident	48	passage	64 sitting
33	utterly	49	immediate	65 trigger
34	surrounding	50	assume	66 professional
35	darkness	51	cellar	67 villain
36	pebbles	52	offensive	68 necessary
37	puddles	53	smell	69 attitude
38	muddy	54	coffee	70 motto
39	eventually	55	puzzled	71 opportunity
40	arrived	56	occupant	72 message

Doubling decisions

dimly, showed, really, started, beginning, slowly, hardly, failure/failing, crossed, grabbed, recording, falling, looked, traveling, singing, hearing, cheering, opening, greatest, feeling, staying, flipping, sipping, spotted, mobbed, quitting, older, stepping, letting, getting, thinner, scrapped, jamming, deepest, dropping, forgetting, remaining, bigger

Problem patterns

1	deterred	deterring	deterrent
2	fittest	fitting	fitfully
3	opener	opening	openness
4	modeled	modeling	
5	occasional	occasionally	
6	hopped	hopping	
7	commoner	commonest	commonness
8	batter	batted	batting
9	forgettable	forgetting	forgetful
10	committee	committing	commitment
11	occurred	occurring	occurrence
12	crueller cruelty	cruellest	cruelly
13	stardom	starred	starring
14	commissioner	commissioning	
15	deferred deferrable	deferring	deferment
16	happening	happened	

Pages 26-27

Noun or verb?

1 He had devised a cunning plan.
2 I advised her not to give up trying.
3 Whoever devised the alarm clock was very clever. It is a useful device.
4 A clairvoyant prophesied my future, but I will be surprised if her prophecy comes true.
5 She took absolutely no notice of my excellent advice.

Sound-alike

weather, foul, meet, past, two, already, waved, saw, wait, missed, course, pouring, wandered, beach, grown, seen, compliment, dyeing, hair, told, whole, stories, aloud, bored, know, lesson, alter, may be, so, sure, led, ensure, write, stationery, piece

Pages 26-27 continued

Can you do better?

SPORT Ike is skillful on the football field and in the swimming pool.

MUSIC More self-discipline and practice are necessary, but Ike has a good sense of rhythm.

DRAMA IKE ENJOYS BOTH TRAGEDY AND COMEDY AND IS A TALENTED CHARACTER ACTOR.

MATH Ike has benefitted from attending extra classes. He has definitely improved, but still makes faults through carelessness.

GEOGRAPHY Ike's project on equatorial rain forests was very knowledgeable.

SCIENCE Ike is uninterested in science and loses concentration easily. He also displays a tendency to talk. During practical work in the laboratory he meddles with the equipment. His techniques are very disappointing.

HISTORY Ike has a thorough understanding of the Ancient World, especially of the lives of the Roman emperors. He has enjoyed learning about the gods and goddesses of Greek mythology.

ENGLISH Although Ike makes little errors in his grammar, his creative writing is generally excellent. His descriptions are perceptive and often humorous. We have been grateful for his assistance in the library this year. As usual, Ike is top of the class at spelling.

Can you get *there*?

1   Look! **There's** Michelle!
2   Look at that, over **there**!
3   I know **they're** going away today.
4   **Their** house is huge.
5   I want one just like **theirs**.
6   **There's** been a dreadful accident.
7   Drop it! It's **theirs**.
8   **There's** been a snowfall overnight.
9   I liked **their** friends.
10 Have some more. **There's** plenty left.
11 I hate going **there**.
12 **They're** always arguing.

Acknowledgements

Series editor: Jane Chisholm
Cover designer: Nicola Butler
Editorial assistance: Fiona Patchett
Americanization editor: Carrie Armstrong